Bend, Break

poems by

Robert Pfeiffer

Plain View Press
P.O. 42255
Austin, TX 78704

plainviewpress.net
sb@plainviewpress.net
512-441-2452

Copyright © 2011 Bob Pfeiffer. All rights reserved under International and Pan-American Copyright Conventions. No part of this book may be reproduced or distributed in any form or by any means, or stored in a data base or retrieval system, without written permission from the author. All rights, including electronic, are reserved by the author and publisher.

ISBN: 978-1-935514-14-5
Library of Congress Number: 2010940941

Cover photo: Erin Kolmodin
Cover design by Susan Bright

Acknowledgements

"Specimens," *The Hurricane Review*, February, 2010; "Cutter" and "The Mole People" *Iconoclast*, February, 2010; "The Reasonable Thing to Do," *The Concho River Review*, May 2009; "Rat Trap," *The Flint Hills Review*, 2009; "God's Work," *The Blue Collar Review*, April, 2008; "Cinderella Sweeping Up," *Black Book Press*, February, 2008; "A Slaughter of Earthworms," *Hidden Oak*, October, 2007; "Where I Go When I Go for a Drive," *Freefall*, June 2007; "Gone" *The Red Owl Magazine*, June, 2007; "The Long Goodbye" *The Naked Knuckle*, October 2006; "The Slowest Suicide," *Twilight Musings*, December, 2005.

This book is for my wife, Echo –

quite simply, there are no words.

Contents

The Kite   9

The Kite	11
The Mole People	13
Treading Backwards Down the Path	14
Urban Frost	15
Pigeons	16
Rat Trap	17
Standing Outside the Hospital at Night	18
Gone	19
Warning Labels	20
Letter to Myself at 20	21
The Night They Served Adam Canola Oil	22
Karmic Whack-A-Mole	23
The Slowest Suicide	24
Crane Scaling	25
Driving With Josh After Rehab	27
Blackwell's Island	28
The Fall of the Shit-House Writer	29
Specimens	30
Mailbox Baseball	31
Photo Album	32

The Sound the Wind Makes   33

The Sound the Wind Makes	35
The Plunge	36
A Slaughter of Earthworms	37
Insomniac Towers	38
Lawn Care	39
All Tomorrow's Parties	40
Cinderella Sweeping Up	41
Finding Certainty	42
Left Behind	43
Major Chords, Minor Notes	44
Cutter	45
The Long Goodbye	46
Armistice Day	47
Schumann Unwound	48
Landlord	50
Step Right Up	51

God's Work	52
Another Fourth	54
Airport '07	55
The Reasonable Thing to Do	56
Duty	57
Shopping Cart	58
Summer Work	59
To A Spider Climbing a Skyscraper	60
Poor Columbus	62
Five Star Service	63
Lacan in the Cardio Room	64
Going to Bed	65

The Long Flight Home — 67

Passing Florence, South Carolina	69
No Reunion	70
Epithalamion	71
Tooth-Brushing: A Love Poem	72
Pain	73
Divorce	74
Driftwood	76
Rose Valley	77
Perrigo Park	78
Office Hours	79
Fishing Off the Jersey Shore	80
Impala	82
Fetal, Skeletal	83
Dung Beetles	84
Robben Island	85
Wine Tasting	87
The Long Flight Home	88
Where I Go When I Go for a Drive	89
The Snow-Bound House	91
About the Author	93

"I did not know what was happening in my heart."

Robert Penn Warren

The Kite

The Kite

Yesterday was beautiful, and so today
we have around us the remnants –
empty beer cans, cigarette butts,
picnic blankets and folding chairs,
styrofoam coolers that no one wanted
to lug back to the car. The city is a mess.

It's grey, the rain having just stopped.
I look out my window, across the street,
at the roof-top level of a parking garage –
all concrete, so much grey. But a red kite
is snagged by the string on a lamppost.

At first, it looks just like a bright bird –
the way it arcs at the edge of some sphere,
reminds me of a Red-tail hawk I saw,
or maybe imagined, baring its shoulders
across the sky just above the tree line.

Then, when the frills along its side
quiver and it moves slowly upward,
it becomes a fish in an aquarium,
red scales reflecting the lances of sun,
making its tenuous way to the surface,
praying for just one more flake to drop.

It scythes down violently like an airplane
that's lost power, and drifted through
that dreaded silence, finally falling
everyone on board already unconscious.
The wind rises, it snaps up, pauses,
then shakes down like a dead leaf.

Continued

I wonder, if the wind blows hard enough,
will the string snap? I like to think
that it would be carried softly away,
on some jet stream that I know doesn't exist,
some miraculous wind tunnel formed
by the exact shapes of all of these skyscrapers.
I know that won't happen. It would just fall.
It would be just like someone's unwanted kite.

My wife comes in, says it looks beautiful –
that bright red, with so much grey around.
How long do you think they'll leave it up there?
she asks. You can only hope for forever.

The Mole People

Beneath the sidewalks, the Mole People scurry
through tunnels they hope are abandoned –
so dark your eyes may never adjust –
they like it that way. We are not welcome here.
They left us above, with our laws and conveniences,
and headed into the gaping mouths
where subways become Els. Down here,
it is blind freedom that drives them –
some to their needles and bottles,
surfacing only for food and fixes –
Some, seeking safety in numbers,
flock to tribes, subterranean hierarchies
that have managed to tap the city's water,
burn fires for warmth and stand guard
in shifts for marauding thieves and thugs.
But it is those others, those that stay deepest –
that are the true masters of this city –
whose pupils distend their corneas,
whose flesh needs no pigment,
who have learned to hunt rats bare-handed,
to break them, skin them, skewer them
lengthwise and feast on them,
who can move, without sound,
within inches and you would never know –
they have become black folded into black.
We leave them to their great concrete veins.

Treading Backwards Down the Path

From here, the city sprawls
like an old man yawning,
stretching its arms for miles
to the north and south. The El
rumbles by every quarter hour
and tonight's mistake is downstairs –
thighs scissoring a crumpled sheet.
There are no more beers to drink.
Right now, out there, people
are mopping marble floors and offices
for strangers they'll never meet.
In my house, traffic jams of books
go nowhere, and frame a television
that drones on low most nights.
The sun is not far off now – soon
she will have to get up, slink out
and pretend there was no last night.
Then maybe I can crawl back
into the cool of my sheets and quilt –
that amniosis – ignore the phone
and pray no prying knock ever comes.

Urban Frost

> *Now am I free to be poetical?*
>   *Line removed by Robert Frost from "Birches."*

They're gouging the earth on all sides –
great, yellow, diesel-powered prehistoria
grunting and chomping dirt and asphalt.
You must always dig down, it seems,
to erect something substantial; to build
behemoths from poured concrete,
stretching to punch a hole in the sky.
You need at least five stories below
ground-level, like planting a fence-post
and packing the dirt around the sides,
enough to hang the birch-fence and not worry
about the wind. And when they're done –
when the armies of workers finally pack
their lunch-pails, pile in their cars and make
their way home to a beer, and a ballgame on TV,
people will never know they were ever here,
never try to imagine the million increments
making up this condo, or that corner office.
Where there was nothing, they dug a hole,
and from that hole worked painstakingly
toward the skies, slowly upward for years.
So now and again, when the sun blisters
the sidewalks, I like to duck inside to feel
the blast of the immaculate air conditioning,
hear my footfalls on the polished marble lobby,
pretend I belong and take the elevator up
all the way to the rooftop, gaze out over
the city, get away from the earth awhile,
and try to imagine what it must feel like
to build something strong enough to stay.

Pigeons

Rats with wings, they brand you –
because you deface our statues,
and rather than peck at the stigma
of canary-yellow flowers, you feast
on the fetid corpse of garbage bags.
You soar from the menacing black
of subway tunnels, and waddle
amongst us as we wait at crosswalks.
Scourge of the city! They curse
those who feed you – spilling seed
in front of benches like a blessing.
They don't think twice when cars
throttle you, leaving you smeared
on the asphalt, barely recognizable,
wing-feathers twisting in the wind.
But they can't see you right now –
how the sun, a falling blood orange,
has caught the oils on you back and
somehow, burst you into rainbow.

Rat Trap

Like some kitten's wind-up plaything,
a rodent scuttles frantically
inside the transparent plastic
trashcan on the subway platform.
His peppercorn eyeballs bulge,
desperate for a sliver of light to crawl through.
He hops, nosing a rip in the bag that hangs
over him like a dying balloon.
If not for the bolts, I could've lifted
his sentence, set him free,
but someone, somewhere along the line
decided that refuse must not be stolen.
And so, as I slide away downtown
I stay fixed on that trapped rat
as he grows smaller to gone.
And I imagine his nose, cold and damp,
spilling his last breaths against the plastic
like tufts of fine cotton.

Standing Outside the Hospital at Night

Notice the snow falling – silent.
And the tumult from the highway,
two blocks behind you, mutes
the flurried exchange between the EMTs
and the doctors – everything is present.

It hardly seems strange – you can't hear
the sirens that carve through the black air
as the ambulance lights circle and flash,
revealing ephemeral corners and alleys
just long enough to realize you missed them.

This urban labyrinth that funneled you
here, its colossal walls towering above
and over you, leads nowhere, has no end.
*There is no jewel on a satin pillow, no fruit
to be plucked from a metaphor, or a tree.*

But, you can send yourself floating
through the corner window on the 7th floor,
the one with the pale, alien light of a television
and a sleeping child, no more than ten,
head smooth as a distant sand dune.

And despite the devastating breath of a respirator,
and the footsteps from some unseen nurse
that resound in the distant hallways,
you might just notice a look on his face, soft
and magnanimous, foreign to you now.

Gone

In the winter, we would mow
croquet courses in the snow –
swing mallets, dig horseshoe
pits and heave the cold steel
until all the beer was gone.

These were full and frequent
days for us; we'd set fire
to the charcoal around noon,
to the couches by midnight
and to our minds in between.

We could hardly drag our asses
out of bed, but could motivate
enough to splice speaker wire,
run it through walls and out windows –
never interrupting the soundtrack.

Some of us are just historians,
scribes, documenting the absurd.
Where can we possibly find reason
or explanation now that so many of us
are wearing tombstones for top hats?

Warning Labels

Now, flying has become an issue –
and I've looked over that list,
ridiculously small on the back
of the bottle, all the adverse
possibilities; no mention of
Panic attacks after take-off.

Now that I think about it,
nothing was in those pamphlets
in the various waiting rooms
all littered with old magazines
and people you tried to avoid –
May cause light-headedness.

It was never even brought up
as a possibility lying on the couch;
countless hours in the shadow
of pastoral paintings, windows
into a world you *should* want –
Upset stomach, dry mouth.

The pills are ingested daily
and manic celebrations replace
the pity-binging and limit-testing.
You build occasions out of nothing,
reasons to remember the days –
Do not take with alcohol.

Warning labels say what not to do,
but nothing about the fear's that come
of mid-air collisions, or engine failure
and the silence before that last sound,
now that you don't want it anymore.
Loss of appetite, fear of the inevitable.

Letter to Myself at 20

Pull your head out of your ass – things are
not as bad as you make them out to be.
But all that rehearsal for misery
will be helpful somewhere down the road.
You've already mastered the sulking amble,
and that abyss you've somehow poured
into your eyes keeps our closest friends
up at night. Thank you – believe it or not.

What I want to say is that I can't stand you –
You're a constant burden, and those notes
you left for me to find, like festering sores
in the margins of all my favorite books
have grown tiresome. You bore me –
nobody's buying your act – the drunken
artist shtick has been done to death.

Oh, and when that miserable February
night rolls around and, in your stupor,
you debate whether to go to the bar
where you know your ex is – don't.
No one cares what you have to say,
No one ever cared what you had to say,
and really, no one ever *will* – I certainly don't.

Anyway, good luck, and buckle-up my man.
The shit has yet to even begin hitting the fan.
.

The Night They Served Adam Canola Oil

The night they served Adam canola oil
I left him a million miles behind,
floating on an ottoman, drifting
in the living room of a cheerleader.

We were out of place anyway – earlier
that night we'd obsessed over hair gel
and exactly how much shirt to tuck in.
We debated the validity of the *condom jinx*.

When Amanda, Kat and Montana slunk
through the oblivious crowd, around
the dance-pop cacophony into the kitchen,
I watched their insidious giggling.

They brought us cold bottles of beer,
and we thanked them, not noticing
the small circle of seniors that formed.
We feigned nonchalance and sipped

With the bitter slide of lager down my throat,
I glimpsed Adam to my left – the victim
of a practical joke from evil girls – oil instead of beer.
His fragile eyes failed him and collapsed.

I was whisked off with the cackling herd
and the quarterback put his arm on my shoulder,
and I saw Adam folding into himself,
doubled over like a pigeon in the rain.

Karmic Whack-A-Mole

Some days it's just better
to keep below the rim,
out of sight, to play it safe –
lest a furious foam hammer
come screaming through
the atmosphere, crashing
hard upon your thick,
synthetic, unsuspecting head.

Other days you jut your chin,
stare ahead, unblinking, and
breathe deep this frenzied circus,
never even suspecting
what will surely be coming
down in vengeful hands
for some long-forgotten fuck up.

The Slowest Suicide

I could do something grand.
I could launch myself into the night:
a Roman Candle exploding,
embers firing, then fizzling
under the friction of the black and rising wind .

Instead, staring into the amber eye of a pint,
I have again chosen the slowest of suicides –
mining rocks from the caverns of my heart,
meticulously stacking them in rows,
different orders, constantly rearranging,
patching the walls whenever they tumble,
searching for that one, perfect design:
intricate pyramids and stately mausoleums,

maybe even a pub ... dark and smoky,
not too different from this one –
but fashioned with the finest acoustics,
stone walls that echo the faint fingering
of Birdman on his impossible tenor sax;
or the scratching of red *Bics* racing
across blank pages like the dogs of hell.

And so, living in the time that God has failed,
I stand and check the new holy trinity:
Wallet... Keys... Cell..., Wallet... Keys... Cell...,
I wade through the mercurial hours
and back up the stairs into the mustard fog.

Crane Scaling

What was it about that great phallus
that you just couldn't resist?
You must've planned it for weeks –
scoped out what time the security guard
made his slow rounds about the site,
double checked the height of that fence,
hoped your old woven welcome-mat
would keep the barbed-wire from slicing
into your palms, or worse, your crotch
as you scissored your way over
and down onto that loud gravel crunch.
Was it just as you'd imagined it?
You'd perfected running crouched over
in dreams as a kid – a Green Beret
infiltrating some secret POW camp –
and when you made it to the base
of the crane, to the door you knew
would be there, you slid bolt cutters
from your backpack and clipped
the padlock like picking grapes
in some abandoned vineyard.
Halfway up, you were noticed –
the impotent guard never gave chase,
just hollered before calling the cops
while you continued your ascent.
And when the world finally arrived –
the police bullhorn muted by distance
and the rush of blood inside your head,
the news helicopters trying to pin you down
with their frantic spotlights, you crept
your way further out that brontosaur neck,
crawling on all fours like a scared dog.
And when the time was finally right,
when you had made it all the way out,
you grabbed hold of that last rung,

Continued

took one deep breath, closed your eyes
and lowered yourself down, swinging free
from those mammoth monkey bars.
Below your feet, twenty stories of nothing.
And you, ignoring your one close-up
from the ocean of news cameras, tears
streaking down your contorted face, laughing
maniacally, like a child in the shore breakers.

Driving With Josh After Rehab

Busted for holding smack in a school zone,
Josh went up on a five year bid –
out in three for good behavior.
I hadn't seen him since, but now he's slouched
in my passenger seat fidgeting with the radio
like nothing sounds good anymore.
He's talking about JV basketball glory days
and senior prom hook-ups, and all the miles
we burned on "Fall Tour," swindling tickets
and slinging cigarettes and grilled cheese
in the parking lots for gas and joint money.
He wears his sobriety like a Purple Heart,
tells me "methadone's a bitch" but he's doing well –
a cush 9 to 5 as a bank teller and a girl called Sally
who stuck by him while he was on the inside.
Inside – that's where he bites his tongue.
I've heard nothing about cellmates or card games;
nothing about that immense "clang"
of the sliding steel door his first night in;
not a word about the stench inside
the flop-house he squatted in for months.
When I glance over at Josh, I don't see
a man with an *inside*; can't see my friend
in his basketball uniform or a rented tuxedo;
can't imagine him dancing on the amphitheater lawn.
All I see is that face – the last one he showed me:
glazed, translucent flesh and hollow eyes
looking back at me, telling me not to worry.
It's really coming down now – I can't see
the rain drops, but I know they're falling
because the wipers squeak back and forth,
trying their damnedest to wipe it all away.

Blackwell's Island

Teetering on the edge of Blackwell's Island,
toeing the East River, the Lunatic Asylum
stands alone, as far away from the city as possible.
Shrouded in river fog and the nothingness
of its background, it seems almost as lost
as the patients inside, whose bare feet and ankles
disappear up into their soiled white gowns.
They waft down the cavernous hallways,
unwatched and left to their own devices.
The manics rave through the hollow night –
they wretch and claw their flesh; while others
lie still, as if restrained, and stare upward,
their eyes like new moons in their sockets.
From the far corner of the third floor comes
a dull, insistent *thud* as some derelict charges
skull-first into his cell wall, then recoils,
then charges again – trying either to end it all
or just to feel something; while in Manhattan,
businessmen swill coffee and check stock-quotes.

The Fall of the Shit-House Writer

It probably got him laid a few times –
moving by night, scrawling love poems,
or suicide sonnets on the dry-erase boards
that lined the halls of our freshmen dorm.

Nobody knew who he was, but I
imagined him in a feathered fedora,
slinking past security to profess himself
eternally, via marker, to a girl he'd only seen.

We dubbed him "The Shit-House Writer"
for the snippets of rhyming philosophy
he left for all to ponder and accept
on the walls of the Men's Room stalls.

A trip to the bathroom often revealed
a recapitulation of Nietzsche in couplets:
You will never truly love and give
Unless it is with danger that you live.

But word spread around campus fast,
novelty turned, as it always does,
to resentment – the artists: jealous,
the women: nervous, the janitors: furious.

And then one day, he was simply gone.
I like to imagine him now, scouring
every square inch of his life for a canvas,
somewhere to spill out onto the world.

Specimens

We were required, by threat
of a failure, to participate
in the time-honored tradition:
"The Middle-School Insect Project,"
to prepare for what comes next.

Armed with only white nets
on slender poles, we scoured
our mortgaged little worlds –
backyards, basements, attics –
for adequate specimens.

Insects trapped in the silken net
entanglements, were transferred
to mason jars. Cotton balls soaked
in poison assaulted futile brains,
filled them up, fogged them in.

And when the insidious cotton
had done its duty, the last twitch
ticked out of skeletal legs –
they were pinned down rigid,
spaced out evenly.

We pierce abdomens with pins,
splay wings wide like petals,
and label phylum, genus, species,
in the ecological verisimilitude
that is an old Nike shoe-box.

Mailbox Baseball

Ankle-deep in empty Pabst cans,
lighting cigarettes but not yet inhaling,
a white-knuckle grip on the side of the pickup,
we careened down country roads in the country dark
with the headlights off.

Coiled in the bed of the Tacoma,
a Louisville Slugger in hand,
we'd swing for the fences
sending mailboxes tumbling,
hurling letters into the air like paper birds.

With a full count and the bases loaded,
a voice thundered through the trees
like a shotgun slug from a house:
Stop! – We peeled out, praying
no one could catch our license plate.

Now, those Pabst cans are imported bottles,
there are white powder stitches on this mirror
and we take our cuts on the inside.
The voices that come – the phone, a knock –
limp through the room, fading just beyond my ears.

Photo Album

We are merely foreground –
The boy at the end of the plaid couch
on my fifth birthday holds a box
wrapped with a blue ribbon –
I don't know his name anymore.
That second knuckle caught
in the frame when we were snapped
in front of the elephant herd
seems disembodied from our safari guide now,
in my memory, there is only a distant accent.
There's a child on a Big-Wheel
in the driveway behind our picnic,
a nephew, I think, dressed like Batman,
pedaling through an imagined Gotham
where there were things still worth saving;
And in the last pages we stand
snaking an arm around each other,
toasting the cool, salt air.
Beyond our leathering skin,
a stranger peeks over his shoulder,
coy as a cartoon villain.
He cranes his wrist and pricks
a middle finger straight through
the fluttering aperture of the moment.

The Sound the Wind Makes

The Sound the Wind Makes

When the kick ball got away,
vanished into the woods
at the base of the hill
behind his house,
he was brave enough to go.

Just six or seven trees deep,
the air became thick,
pulled him to a slow stop
like an anchor dragging
through a river-bottom.
The leaves that remained
on the branches swayed,
droned like an army of locusts.
The back of his neck grew cold,
sending charges to his tips.
His eyes glazed and blurred,
so he was only vaguely aware
of that sound the wind makes
filling his ears like plaster,
and he couldn't hear the table
breaking far behind him then,
or his mother's screams,
or a little later, the sirens.

The sound the wind makes
when it blows through the trees
can infest the trunks of children,
stick to their ribs and hide –
keeping dormant for decades
some fracturing rumor of pain.

The Plunge

When pigeons take the plunge
they fall like black hail
from far-off window ledges.
They plummet four or five stories,
deploy their feathered chutes
and start a parabolic glide,
indifferent, towards another perch.

When we try to do the same,
take that lemming leap –
a clumsy kiss in back of the school bus,
or that first acrid sip of dad's beer –
we fall hard, and pick up speed.
Through this graveyard fog
it's clear we don't all have chutes.

A Slaughter of Earthworms

I didn't even notice them until
I was right in the middle of it –
there was a minor incongruity
in an otherwise unremarkable step
in the walk to the 10th St. subway:

Something under my middle toe
resisting its insignificance,
pushing up a little harder than the rest,
causing me to lift my foot and swing
it to the side, clearing a view.

There, laying crisply against gray
concrete slates as if pinned down
and labeled in a child's science project –
the burnt corpse of an earthworm
curled into itself like a rusty fishhook.

With only the slightest refocusing,
of my eye, there was another –
and another still, and as my sight
grew wider, there were hundreds,
thousands of fatal miscalculations.

They only wanted to make it across
the sidewalk from the flower bed
to the grass or visa versa, who knows?
Perhaps the sun came up too fast today
catching them off guard, a sneak attack.

More likely, the sun rose as it usually does,
slow and red, and each one took its shot.
Some made it, others not even half way –
and now these coiled, brittle metaphors
freckle the pavement into faces I have known.

Insomniac Towers

There are only a few of us sane enough
to be awake at a quarter to four,
blasting halogen flares
out of living room window panes.

Birch trees rise from the courtyard
between and below us – we surround them
and they scrape gently against the wind
weaving some idiotic safety net.

There's the alcoholic divorcé – in his underwear
drinking brown liquor with ice.
He lounges in a recliner, fondling
his remote, flipping it lengthwise in his palm.

Below him, a woman on her treadmill,
runs hard toward the sliding glass door.
There's a breakfast table and matching chairs
on her balcony. She lives alone.

Bleary eyed, I remember road trips,
trying to catch the face of someone passing
in another car and wanting to become,
if only for a moment, that stranger's eyes.

Someone sliced the ears off of nighttime,
leaving us alone and mute, awash
in the onslaught of infomercials,
and white noise.

Lawn Care

Under a bone-colored sky,
my neighbor revs his leaf-blower –
it must be November.
Every year he relishes this –
blasting diesel-powered wind
through the plastic barrel,
moving his arm back and forth
like he's hunting for arrowheads,
making yellow and red waves
rise in the air and then crash
until his driveway and walks are bare.
But now our cul-de-sac is littered
with what was once only his concern.
When December comes gusting,
I know those leaves will be mine.
Then I'll get down my leaf-blower
from the attic and tug at the starter
like I'm yanking at some tough root.

All Tomorrow's Parties

A tranny with a spike in his arm
slouches like a fabulous wet towel
on Warhol's brilliant red couch.
The silver walls of the Factory
reflect spastic strobe flashes
across the dance floor. Brando rides
his silkscreen Harley, and Jackie-O
smiles coy through blue mascara.
Reds and blow course through
blood streams, spin skulls behind
cigarette smoke and Ray-Bans.
The blonde with the feather boa
and the strap-on dildo flings paint
and shattered glass at a canvas
stretched out on the floor. She came
from Kansas on a Greyhound,
desperate to become something
beautiful – came to this satellite of ice
hurtling recklessly through neon.

Cinderella Sweeping Up

Tonight she has let me stay late
because I promised to help
stack the chairs on the tables
and because we've gotten to know
one another, and she's never
had to deny me her number
or a night of clumsy grasping
at brassiere hooks, or button flies,

She never shows her teeth,
even to smile at a big tipper.
She will not open her mouth
to laugh, even at my best jokes.
She won't talk about her ex,
and always walks in shadows
that never manage to hide
the arcane depth of her eyes.

She tallies her receipts, listening
to the juke box softly playing
her songs and she sings words
that are slightly off, but just fine.
In two years, after she graduates
she says she'll come back here,
sit in a booth and enjoy the most
expensive thing on the menu.

It's now two hours since the last drunk
got up and stumbled out the door,
and her yellow broom bristles
on the stale but sticky concrete,
pushes stubbed cigarettes, ashes
and wet crumpled napkins
into faultless minor mountains –
from this, she shapes a better world.

Finding Certainty

When it comes to making
you feel like a piece of shit,
not much can top time
spent with real-job people,
basking in a plunge-pool,
overlooking the Pacific.

They know the first names
of the chefs in 5-star restaurants –
places you could never go
and define their annual salaries
as percentages of a million.

Then, on the flight back,
there's the *Customs* form,
and the sober anxiety
that comes with filling out
the employment section –
a sigh - *student/writer*.

But redemption might come
that first early morning home
as she sleeps on her side –
you notice the snow-covered
hillside of her shoulder.

Left Behind

Lying between metal rails –
a syringe, plunger plunged,
and a metal spoon, mangled
to an "S," burnt to bronze
on its swollen, convex belly.

Perhaps the arm that was stuck
by this needle is attached
to the body that left behind
the pile of human remnants
which festers on the landing
one and a half stories below
the street on which hundreds
are enjoying their happy-hour.

Maybe the blistered hand
that held the spoon so many times
is the hand that now nervously
flicks open closed open closed
a metal Zippo across from me,
as we are pulled methodically
through the veins of our city.

More likely, the body that holds
the blood which was sucked
into that plastic barrel, mixed
then injected, is the corpse
of a man found frozen yesterday
on the downtown monument
of the Great Seal of Georgia –
a horizontal disc of state pride.
From a block away, it was said,
he looked like nothing more
than a roach on a birthday cake.

Major Chords, Minor Notes

Approaching thirty and imbibing
yet another college buddy's nuptials,
I was sitting with mostly strangers –
bride's cousin on her father's side,
uncle Stu and his new boyfriend.
I stared at the scattered remains
on my buffet plate: a few shrimp tails,
half a roll, trimmed ham fat with gravy.
I wasn't looking to remember anything
in particular, or to crawl back up
the greasy garbage chute of time,
but then it happened –
the band was strumming a cacophonous finale
and the sound was swelling inside me
and suddenly I am in a C chord
walking it down to an A minor.
The air is soaked with sweet tobacco
and we are all here, all piss and vinegar,
cold beers sweating in the just evening sun.
Someone is tending the barbeque, taming
the flames that rasp the burgers and dogs
and smoke the sun red,
and the laughter is immense,
the joy is too much, crushing us
and then, as quickly as it came, it dissolved.
I was back in the cavernous hall
where the first brave and drunk souls
stumbled their way out onto the dance floor,
while I escaped to this lavish patio
to strike up a ceremonial cigar.
The calm breeze from the waves crashing
throttles my last match to a damp spark –
a whisper of smoke only curls and fades.

Cutter

The scars look like switchbacks
traversing her from wrist to shoulder.

But she was never beaten – her father
didn't take his time while bathing her

when she was a girl; she was loved
often, and in all the appropriate ways.

She didn't trade 60 watt for black light,
never pierced anything other than ears;

in high school she was a cheerleader,
then a sorority girl with a double major.

It's nothing you'd expect – she just likes
the way it feels when a fresh razor eases

it's way in, how the burgundy cascades,
pooling ever so slightly on the rough

ledges of her flesh – she imagines them
as battle scars – proof of a struggle unseen.

She presses the blade, delicate as surgery.

The Long Goodbye

The pepper-flecked scoop of eggs,
has gone cold. It sits next to stale
toast, a pat of butter and a six-ounce,
plastic thimble full of orange juice
from concentrate, now room temperature.

Behind them, in her chair, she fixates
on the smudge-marks on her window
that partially blur her only view –
of that bird-feeder that dangles
from the lowest branch of the oak tree,
unwavering in the center of the garden.

Greeting cards line the sealed fireplace,
offering their usual pastel well-wishes.
The rest of the room is vacant, save
for a few framed pictures of family
and decorative bells on the dresser.

She hears voices like distant foghorns,
stares through her nursing-home room,
as empty as the only look she can give
my father, the son she no longer remembers.

Armistice Day

Your brittle, yellow poems –
half a century in an envelope
in a hat box, in a dusty attic –
suffering through two generations
of sweltering South Carolina
summers – an attempt to forget
what was done to remember.

There is a texture to words
when articulated with a typewriter,
almost engraved in ivory paper –
a permanence otherwise lacking.
There is personality in the lines,
mechanical penmanship: the way
the lower case *a*'s in *Stalag Luft 3*
stand slightly above the rest
like guards in that watchtower.

When I hold this paper to my face,
I smell the fuel, hear the deafening
clamor of the bomber engines,
feel it shuddering in my ribcage –
And although I will never know
the taste of stale, black bread
after three impossible years of nothing
else – whether the texture would trigger
a gag, or if maybe the hunger was such
that you could turn it into buttered biscuits –
even now I can taste those caramel chews
that you would give me years later
from that glass jar beside your chair.

Schumann Unwound

Like spastic little grackles
Schumann's mad hands fluttered,
lifted all the way from his loins as if hoisting
the whole building above his head
like some primitive sacrifice. He paused –
then slashed down, trusted baton
severing symphony from eardrum.

But in the best theaters
that last note floats like a ghost,
audience breathless, musicians flexed,
and when it finally fades
there is only the illusion of silence –
a singular moment devoid of shuffling
until the crowd rips into applause.

It would surge through him like a bruising tide
when Schumann turned and bowed.
Then one night, perched and throbbing,
when finally the audience ebbed,
he bowed once more but something stayed –
the last note of the evening
hanging on – persistent like boxed ears.

That A-minor hung, mounted like a portrait
until the next last note, then *that* one
through the next – through hallways,
through voices, dinners and dreams,
always somehow there, always eating at him
until he could no longer conduct
and launched himself into the icy Rhine.

I wonder if there was only that note inside
his head on the long walk to the bridge.
Were there stable-coaches passing by
on muted cobble-stone? Did strangers call to him,
their words only A-minor? I wonder
if he could even hear that devastating gurgle,
sinking down, of the bubbles rising to surface.

Landlord

This morning it's winter in springtime,
but I don't have gloves for these shaking fingers.
Regardless, I'll stand on this sidewalk all day
leaning into my pockets, breathing smoke signals,
and wait for my tenants to pass me by
on their walk to the subway, or the bus stop.
Some will hold their children tighter
or cross the street when they see me drink
beer for breakfast. No shave, no shower.
Then, around noon, when the fridge gets bare
I'll walk a few blocks to the corner store –
two birds – exercise *and* supplies.
We have, my tenants and I, an agreement –
I cut 'em some slack when their rent is late
so they'll look the other way when I'm too lit
to fix the hot water, or when I'm passed out
in the hallway and they've got company –
it's a real, human-level arrangement.
No, no one *dreams* of a life like this –
rotting teeth, yellow eyes, dank basement –
level apartment with one dangling bulb.
But still, at night, I set my breathing
to my father's old, bronze metronome,
and sink into my ragged reading chair,
admiring this spectacular malaise,
the victrola whispering Brahms as I search,
bleary-eyed, for patterns in the TV snow.

Step Right Up

When the smell of corn dogs frying floats
across the fairgrounds and hangs low
in the air like a stale balloon; when the whir
of the ferris wheel snaps on and hums its song,
fresh autumn splashing over my face
and I look out over this preposterous
candy-striped wonderland, I know I'm home.
Rust-Belt to Bible-Belt we travel together,
my son and me, running the Ball Toss –
you know, the one where you get five tries
to knock over three milk bottles? Sounds
too easy, huh? But, buddy, that's our racket.
We've got the whole thing down to a science.
We're like artists, me and my boy –
We turn on the country charm, tease
out the twang and rake it in hand over fist.
When the little rug-rats come running up,
fresh off a funnel cake lunch, asking
their granddad to win something for them,
we have them toss at the lighter bottles.
Kids deserve a good time now and again.
But the trouble with kids is they grow up.
So when the sun sets and *you* come here
on your big date after football practice,
trying to win a teddy-bear for the home-
coming queen and hoping to get laid, we switch
to the weighted bottles – might as well be
cemented down – you don't stand a chance.
No sir, you can look at the waft of mustache
on my boy's lip with all the scorn you want,
but you'll be slinking away, tail limp between
your legs. Good luck getting it up tonight!

God's Work

On the front page, Edgar Ray Killen,
a man with a name so fitting
even Hollywood might pause,
sits in his wheelchair –
stone-faced and still untouched.
He is somebody's grandfather –
some little girl's *Paw-Paw*.
The congregation know him
as the kind and gentle type.
He gives candy apples on Halloween.

He has slept well every night
for the last forty-one years
since he rounded up the troops –
all decked out in their wives'
finest bedding, stole the three Yankees
from their car on Rock Cut Road
and watched the beating, and the bullets
that shattered their skulls like china dolls,
then had some pals with bull-dozers
dig a deep grave under an earthen dam.

I was doing God's work, he claimed,
and boasted to the Sheriff (also Klan)
that he knew the boys' last words –
"I know how you feel, sir."
And even though he left the corpses
to rot under the Mississippi earth
for forty-four summer days and nights,
the all-white jury of his close peers
just couldn't convict their preacher.

So now, framed in this picture, so feeble,
tubes looped over his ears and into his nose
from the oxygen tank that sustains him
it's possible to look close, so close
the pixels break from their greater image.
So close you indeed move through
a single pixel and inside the courthouse.
You can smell his wife Betty Jo's perfume;
hear her gasp and whimper at the verdict;
taste those corpses, still rotting today,
and feel no pity at the pathetic sight
of this skeletal man cursing reporters
and the system, as he is finally wheeled,
oxygen tank and all, past Betty Jo,
his grandchildren, and the widows he made.

Another Fourth

As smoke seeps from the pursed lips
of the well-worn charcoal Weber,
and drifts skyward through shivering air,
the coolers grow dangerously empty.

The tons of mammal flesh being charred
this Independence Day should stun
any mind that tumbles the concept –
and there are horseshoes to toss.

Here, the freedoms being celebrated
are a paid vacation, carte blanche
drinking-binges, copious fireworks –
the divine rites of every American Joe.

We stake our claim to various backyards,
curl our toes in well-manicured lawns,
and with a certain, blithe insouciance,
turn our backs on the exploding sky.

Airport '07

They come from all corners,
strangers swooping down
in psychotic parabolas
and leave furiously, even harder.
I sit here at Gate D-23,
waiting for my plane, watching
businessmen heatedly thrusting
through security lines and customs.
Suitcases on wheels push
through clogged arteries to whatever
jetway marks their plans.
So many are going –
some wearing floral shirts,
others bundled up.
How many are going home?
Who's moving someplace new –
butterflies in their guts, minds popping
like freshly dropped Alka-Seltzer?
Reunions are held at baggage claim
and fare-thee-wells at curbside.
The bars are well-peopled before noon,
time zones be damned,
and in front of me, a mother
has her daughter by the wrist,
yanking her toward a final boarding.

The Reasonable Thing to Do

I poured out some beer
because I had seen someone do it
in a movie, or had heard it in a song.
It seemed like the kind of thing
you should do to let others know
that this shit happens all the time;
the kind of thing you do to bury yourself
deep in the gravity of a coda.

When they walked the casket past,
I strained to think of nothing
but the sound the tires must have made
before they hit the curb, jumped
onto wet October grass, hurling the car
fifty miles-per-hour into that maple.
I marked each and every moment,
I owed it to myself to remember it all.

It's been almost ten years now
and even more caskets since that first
unrequited sip splashed over the silver gravel
of our deserted high-school parking lot
and I have tipped and poured a bottle
every single time, without fail
for all the car wrecks, sober and drunk,
for the suicide and the overdoses
for the one on the hundred and fourth floor,
and there is only one thing I have learned:
Save your beer. You're gonna need it.

Duty

On Wednesdays, they come to stroll the park –
the son, whose own sons have daughters now,
on his lunch break, his father with nothing left
to take a break from. The wheelchair creaks,
yellow foam blooms from the cushion –
but at this point, the old man says, *What's done is done.*
The son leans in hard when they climb hills, palms
the sweat from his neck – his father can't help anymore.
He bends down, speaks into the one good ear,
something easy – that brunette's jogging shorts,
how maybe next week they'll bring sandwiches –
no sense angering the day with inevitability.
When they make it back to the rest home,
the father, nodding off, starts to cough.
The son balls a handkerchief to mop up the phlegm
and before goodbye, smoothes the part in his old man's hair.

Shopping Cart

Some say that they'd love nothing more
than to be stuck forever in their teenage years,
when there was still perfect mystery
in the way that sundresses shivered,
and the curves of tan thighs were miracles.
But seeing you buried in my shopping cart,
staring up from underneath my four avocados,
my half-gallon of cranberry juice, framed
on the cardboard side of skim-milk carton,
grinning just as you were two years ago –
all dressed up for school picture day –
I know that your braced smile disappeared
when some meaty palm came down
and ripped you into understanding.
You will still be thirteen next week,
as I walk the aisles hunting for bargains,
and next month as well, until everyone you know
has given up hope. I promise I will find you
a better resting spot, uncovered near the front
with the potato chips and the cage-free eggs.

Summer Work

The thrill had leaked out by mid-July –
I'd hold the pressure washer like a rifle,
blasting the mold from the siding of houses.
T-shirt drenched and wrapped skin-tight,
lower back clenched like an angry fist,
bruised shins from leaning out over
the top step of a ladder to paint the trim.
It had seemed romantic at first: working outdoors,
building calluses like grated pearls on my palms.

But it topped ninety-five for twenty straight days;
even from the shade where I'd take smoke breaks
you could almost see the water inside the air –
so stifling, just staying vertical became the job.
Then my girl left me, blamed the drugs,
but I bet it had more to do with blue-box
mac & cheese dinners four nights a week
and me limping home slimy and bitching
about my pay, with only enough energy
to jot down a few melodramatic lines,
get drunk and paw at her while she slept.

August came in hard, buckling my knees,
and one day with the washer's motor rumbling
and the air stinking of squashed crab apples,
I looked down – eight hairy legs pricking
my forearm, eyes and fangs somehow massive.
My right hand came down without thought,
left four red fingers and a smear of limbs behind.
The air was heavy. I couldn't hear the motor.
The spray was hotter than I'd imagined –
it churned through the meat it meant to clean.
Blood pulsed out – I dropped everything
and ran my index finger through the jagged chasm,
pressing deeper each time, tearing the flesh
at both ends, searching for the solid bone inside.

To A Spider Climbing a Skyscraper

I walk my dogs before the sunrise
behind the "No Pets Allowed" sign,
and, again, stand like the center pole
of some carnival ride as, leashes taut,
they sniff circles around me.
That first morning, it was the glow
from a streetlight which caught
that one silk tightrope,
shivering between a tuft of pine
and someplace outside the light.
You – dime-sized, weighing it down.

The next morning, by some miracle
of evolution or sheer diligence,
you had cast a glass fretwork
over the neighboring condos –
a shattered windshield in the sky.
For about a week, you were there,
and if I was lucky there was light rain,
and your filaments would strain just slightly,
holding onto a single drop like a secret.

I would stand and make a perfect line
between me, you and the building
so you grew into a horrifying beast,
blocking out the glowing squares
of those other few already awake.
If I closed my right eye, you'd shift
four balconies and seem to scale the side,
massive legs lumbering toward the roof.
And if I closed both eyes, I could see
you from inside someone else's home –
their couch, their coffee mug, their life –
your belly hairy, your fangs like tusks.

Until – maybe it was a storm, or the pluck
of a mockingbird, or maybe it was just
the maintenance staff doing their job –
one day I walked down, dogs pulling me
to you once again, and I looked up –
scraping against the black, morning sky,
only the entanglement of the turning leaves.

Poor Columbus

When you ordered the anchors dropped
and your beloved fleet rocked to a halt,
you thought you'd just unearthed
the gaping mouth of the Gihon,
Eden only up river, around the bend.
And we could hardly blame you –
flowers exploding from their stems,
those craggy bluffs that gash the sky,
high enough to avoid any flood.
Anyone could mistake this for Paradise.
But tell us, Christóbal, did it sink you
to discover it was only the Orinoco;
that you could paddle upstream
till your men were blue in the face,
and all there would ever be was strong
current, and ancient, inland Venezuela?

Five Star Service

They come to you with warm towels
at check-in – moist and aromatic;
chilled glasses of freshly squeezed
papaya juice on a burnished platter.

You and your new wife are here
to eat, drink, make love and lie
beneath the sun in the powdered
sugar sand of equatorial paradise.

They will dote on you – genuflect,
bring clean towels, refresh your drinks.
You will think because they laugh
at your jokes, and you tip well,

and ask about the local culture,
that you share something significant –
that they appreciate your sincerity.
The hard truth is: you're nothing

but a tourist. And when you reach
cruising altitude on the flight home,
you will see the dappled shanties –
they etch their lives from your pittance.

Lacan in the Cardio Room

> Jaques Lacan's psychoanalytic theory of the "mirror stage"
> purports that when a young child first sees itself in the mirror,
> it realizes for the first time that it is a finite creature,
> separate from the rest of the world. This is also the
> introduction to the human obsession with body image.

Get ready to pedal backwards –
the display flashes its warning
as the new mother, mid-thirties,
trying to re-claim her teenage thighs,
wheels in the Eddie Bauer stroller
next to an excer-cycle. She positions
her child facing her, then sits down.
She straps her feet in and adjusts
the seat, pulling levers and knobs,
setting the Course and Resistance.
But the child is crying. The mother,
frustrated, mouths to me "Sorry."
She gets up, rolls the stroller over
to the mirrored wall in front of us
and shows the child exactly who
"mama's good little girl" really is.
The baby, now properly propped up,
after another series of adjustments,
cranes it's bulbous head and stares
at that reflection with the wild eyes
of a pygmy owl. The mother starts
her workout again. On the elliptical,
I pump my arms; we charge towards
the greater selves we'll never be.

Going to Bed

Bridge Night is getting smaller –
the group has whittled down.
Faces have begun to fade.

The music is softer now,
but they don't listen much anymore.
They tend to their pleasures.

He, in his leather chair, reads,
bible-sized war histories, mostly.
He fans the pages in front of his nose.

She creeks with the porch swing –
a crossword puzzle fills over hours
with blue ink on her lap like a bath.

They rise, together, to their room,
say goodnight, and leave the unsaid.
They sleep with the windows open.

The Long Flight Home

Passing Florence, South Carolina

I see my mother, swaddled in 1950,
a purple cotton blanket wrapped
to the soft folds under her chin,
eyes shut, nose barely whistling.
That hospital might still be there,
its brick façade slicked with mold,
white-soled sneakers squeaking
through its halls, but I wouldn't know.
She's always been beautiful, my mother –
a squawking pre-teen tom-boy racing
through *kick-the-can* at recess;
at fourteen, dwarfed behind the wheel
of a Corvair, her father teaching her
to shift gears on drought-bit dirt roads;
years later, coming home from college,
russet hair, straight as her convictions,
and down to the waist of her bell-bottoms.
Florence – nestled in the shadow
of the interstate, where I-20 unfurls
from 95 like an asphalt tongue –
I should exit here. I should drive slowly
through the streets of her hometown,
until I see flashes of her at the lake,
swan-diving from a floating dock,
sipping a fountain-pop at a diner counter,
opening her locker to cutouts of Mick Jagger,
riding in the backseat of a convertible,
belting *Tracks of My Tears*, to beat the wind,
until she's here in my passenger seat
drumming her palms on the dash.

No Reunion

You spot her right off the bat –
over by the front door, uncurling
the tendrils of her cashmere scarf –
and you notice that she's cut her hair
to her shoulders and the designer frames
of her eye-glasses suit her fair skin,
soft as you remember. You watch
as she weaves through the crowd,
and sits across the table, chatting
with girlfriends and orders chardonnay.
You wait for her smile, and flash
to that night you held her in the folds
of your parka – your hips touching,
the cinnamon gloss on her lips.
You do not love her. You never did.
But it is something like heartbreak
when she glimpses right past you –
hazel eyes never breaking stride –
and suddenly it dawns on you
that in the so-called prime of your life,
you were nothing worth remembering.

Epithalamion

You took a three thousand mile plunge –
launching from Washington on a whim,
slaloming your way around the jagged spines
of the Cascades, somewhat softened
by the loitering snow, and set your course
to the east with only your one suitcase
and that awful, gut-wrenching freedom
around each next bend in the highway.

The walls of the filing room had begun
their slow, sinister creep inward around me –
shelves packed with little cardboard cubes,
documents therein lovingly arranged by me
in perfect reverse-chronological order –
each box a roadmap to some beginning.
That room – so tidy and quiet – belied
the reality of a life torn from its foundation.

And when you settled here, something
like a tributary exploded in the sky
and the floodgates busted wide open.
Soon the haunting flashes of memory,
once like hulking ravens, pulsing
and threatening to bat their massive wings,
now like long-abandoned birds' nests,
freckling the naked thickets in winter.

Tooth-Brushing: A Love Poem

I love the way the minty foam fills
up your mouth, almost overflowing
those soft lips, and how you only spit out
when you're completely done, just because
that's how you've always done it. I love
your stubbornness. I love how you cup
your palm under the faucet and splash
water around, rinsing the porcelain clean.
I love how, just by listening, I can tell
whether you're making short strokes
on your front teeth, pulling back your lips,
or whether you're reaching far for molars,
which carries a deeper sound than the rest.
But more than anything else, I *love* the way
you hit the bathroom lights, peek out,
then do a half-skip over to our couch,
asking me to rub your head – I feel
like I could break apart when I smell
the shampoo from your sandy-blonde hair
as it cascades over my shoulder onto my chest.

Pain

A silence I didn't notice –
then a sputtering breath
from inside the bedroom –
that jagged verge of panic.
I edge my head past
the doorframe – your face,
folded inside your hands,
buried deep in the down
of your pillow. A slight twitch.
Another. I send out questions –
they return with nothing.
No reaction to the backs
of my fingers as I trace
circles over your temple.
Some ancient burden
is heaving inside you
and all I can offer is my palm
on the small of your back.

Divorce

Two garbage bags and half an hour –
that's what my wife, at twelve, was given.
She thinks now that she knew then –
for months her mother came home late
slipped as silently as those flannel sheets
would allow, into her bed and stared
at the ceiling with eyes that never adjusted,
even after decades, to that mountain dark.

Her parents had moved there young,
in love, perhaps. That first night it was pouring –
the road had washed out at the cattle guard
so they grabbed what they could, and slogged
the three miles up, mud sucking at their heals.
When they crested the top – the mountains
like black sea swells, the towering pines
like monoliths, whispering in the rain –
her mother cried, her father pitched the tent.
In the morning, he dug the foundation.

Years later she would notice the silence,
and the tone of the few words muffled
through the walls, as she curled on her bed
with her books and the worlds she'd create.
Things fall apart – she knew it even then.
So when her father took her brother to Spokane
to buy him a new dirt bike, and her mother
came in with a look she'd never seen, a voice
she'd never heard, she wasn't surprised.

She breaks a little, even now, telling me
how, a couple days later, her father knelt down
in front of her, asked who she wanted to live with.
She said *Mom*. His eyes became wet glass.
I imagine it how it couldn't possibly be –
her palm on the rear windshield, her father
growing smaller. All she remembers is the family
dog, confused, panicked, pawing, at the car door,
yelping after them the whole way down.

Driftwood

Buoyant with insight, I bob
with the swells of Lake Roosevelt,
pondering the pale driftwood stacked
in this sandy cove like piled corpses.
There are oak branches and aspen trunks,
whole pine trees stripped of smaller limbs,
nubs jutting out like arthritic fingers –
all things blown into the Columbia
by strong winds, or swept away by a flood.
But it is our dunnage that seems most out of place –
a kitchen table; a once-stained cabinet door
(it's bronze knob still somehow polished);
a cross-beam which could have spanned
the roof of a hunting cabin, threaded down
through years at one end like a Louisville Slugger,
sticking up from the mangled collection
like the longest point of a Buck's antlers;
one lone oar – I imagine a shipwreck
up in Canada hundreds of years ago,
men in a lifeboat for days, this paddle
finally dropped to the bottom in resignation.
These mere pieces of driftwood – fell
into the river and were brought right here,
to slap at the hull of our fishing boat,
or to leak their water and weight into the sand.
But for the thumbnail-sized frog, it is home.
For the river rat, it is the only shelter
from the hulking bald eagle, who perches
here now, golden beak ticking side to side.
For us, driftwood is far too brittle for function –
no chance at a second life fashioned
as a step-stool or rocking chair – at best,
something decorative for the mantle.
But as the wake from some larger boat swells
beneath me, it seems that it was brought here
to be gathered, and again and again turned over
until it becomes, once more, worth saving.

Rose Valley

Seen from above, fireworks do not explode
as you are used to them doing.
They do not launch high into the night,
clap like thunder, and pulse Technicolor
down on a wide-eyed, expectant crowd.
They do not cast blue then green then red
over the face of your high-school lover –
slowly, at first, then building to that great
incendiary spasm that flits your eyes,
as you both ease into deviant grins.
There's no sense of freedom, as when your dad –
so young in your mind now – disappeared
behind a sand dune with Roman Candles
while you and your brother traced figure 8s
in the air with your Sparklers like swords.
No – from atop Rose Valley, there is nothing
at all magical about this Independence Day.
Just above the surface of Curlew Lake
parachutes of glowing jewels deploy
in a well-charted sequence, each trailing
a distant *Pop*, no louder than a cap-gun.
From a different angle, and far closer,
it all might have appeared as it really is –
awesome, and somehow horrifying –
embers falling, burning as they fall.

Perrigo Park

-For Ben May

The pistol, so much heavier now,
a single round inside the chamber,
rests in his lap, cold and coiled like …
one more connection he can't make.
The car idles. It's been a beautiful day.
The windows down, the radio off –
no more songs. The sound of a breeze,
and over there the alders sway so slightly
that they might not be moving at all.
He gets out, leaves the car running, frays
into the thick underbrush in front of him.
In his mind, an abandoned farm. A single line
of fence-posts bends over the horizon

Office Hours

The hallway smells stale, like tuna sandwiches
lifted from plastic lunchboxes in grade school,
the fluorescent lights flicker and hum above you
and the recycled air sags in the windowless office.
She comes to you during your designated time –
begrudgingly takes out her earphones and smiles,
but can barely hide the disdain behind her teeth.
She sits beside you, and you try to entertain her –
a sarcastic quip about how you're *sure* she's happy
to be there and not outside on her Friday afternoon.
You try to explain the importance of understanding
comma splices, and tense shifts, and of making
a strong argument in more than just her essays.
But behind her dull eyes, only apathy festers –
she thinks you are wasting her time and your life,
and you are not so sure she's wrong. But still,
you slog through the rest of your notes. She leaves,
and you sigh. The next student rounds the corner
wearing the t-shirt of a band you've never heard of,
finishing up a phone call, and you pull his paper, red ink
splashed all over it like a bloodbath. He couldn't care less.

Fishing Off the Jersey Shore

Salt water lapping the bow, not fifty yards
from the dock, jutting out from our summer rental,
green-headed horse flies chomping away
at my singed shoulders, I kept a vigil inside
our little outboard schooner, not much more
than a dinghy, eating the turkey sandwich
that my mother had made, wrapped
in tin foil and brown-bagged for me.
Beads forged on the old silver Thermos
like blown glass, fell and shattered at my feet.
The *rhythm* of it all: up, down, drip, drip, drip.

Then, a bite. The rod snapped forward,
bending over halfway, retching in violent spurts,
testing my grip. I dug in and yanked back,
setting the hook, then fell forward cranking
like my dad taught me, and his father him.
I reared back again and again,
the metal reel burrowing into my palm,
my fingers and forearms on fire,
chest burning with the expectation
of finally having something worth mounting.

It wriggled up like a pale scarf,
close enough to the surface to just make out –
a dorsal fin sliced through the waves
and inside me some primal instinct leapt.
As though from another place I watched
as it was hauled into the boat, and I stumbled
backwards clinging to the gunwale
as the shark thrashed back and forth.
It's head, like a front end of an old Buick,
snapped open and the jaws jutted out
latching onto the wooden club, whipping
it against the side with a thick metallic thud.

A hook pierced through the bottom
of its mouth, ripping the leathery flesh;
its six-inch jaws, a maniacal grin;
blood oozing from the wound.

I had no choice, it seemed, but to jump.
The cold water shocked my skin as I sank
screaming out the terrible bubbles,
flailing my limbs, climbing toward air.
Panicked for anything else that might glide
from the black into the blue below me,
I thrashed towards the safety of our dock,
a dervish of looping arms and whitewater.
I pulled myself up and turned in time
to see the shark somehow launch itself
over the side and disappear, a silver blade
glinting homeward. It struck me,
sitting there, wet as the day I was born,
that I was the one who cast the lure.
The abandoned boat silently rocked.

Impala

We round a corner, night having fallen,
our tracker trains his spotlight
on the brilliant, spotted fur of a leopard
heaving in the tall grass for air,
stuffed to paralysis by her last meal.
The sound of breathing and clicking cameras,
the smell something like road kill.
The beam of light slides along the brush,
up into the branches of a red bushwillow.
There, thirty feet above the jeep,
the mangled corpse of an Impala,
neck snapped at a gruesome angle –
the sign a quick death, we hope –
gutted along the torso, intestines dangling,
he hangs there, and sways just slightly,
like some grisly sweater from a clothesline.

Fetal, Skeletal

It could've been a softball nestled in the back lawn.
It could've been an Easter egg in a wicker basket.
Or maybe a topographical globe waiting for paint.

But there is the fetid stench of decomposition,
and there are two male lions hulking like kings
under the swooning branches of a guarri tree,
a two-ton buffalo carcass, swollen to shining
rises from the bush like a mountain of rotting flesh.

You are nowhere near home. The guide adjusts
the bolt action rifle slung over his shoulder, points
to the quartz-white sphere you can't stop staring at
and, without the slightest affect, says "Fetus' skull."

Turns out the lions can smell what grows inside,
and, sometimes before the mother is completely gone,
will rip it out and eat it, because the meat is tender,
and unborn things are packed with nutrients.

What should haunt you, you think, is how normal
it all seemed at the time. How you were fine,
thrilled, even, with having seen it, because it happened
in *nature* and because you know you'll have pictures
to brag to friends about for decades at dinner parties.

Even still, something planted inside you makes you feel
guilty for not feeling guilty, and so you imagine the sound
of the flies, frenzied, loud as a hurricane, swarming
above the carnage as the jeep lurches to life, lumbers away,
crushing the saplings under its thick, rubber tires
and the vultures in the trees keep their silent vigil.

Dung Beetles

They back out, hind legs kicking
though packed shit toward life.
Their parents roll their birth-houses,
balls of mud and dung for the eggs
and leave them in the dirt, underneath
some brush, half buried if they're lucky.
How strange the fresh air must seem,
how like a miracle that massive sky –
though they will never process anything
beyond instinct. You'd never notice
unless someone told you where to look –
small like rusted pennies, they scamper
through the bush like blown leaves.
They feed on what they come from –
gathering what others have left behind,
rolling it into boulders three times
their size. They throw their weight
into it, like Sisyphus, until they die.
If you look quickly, before the breeze
wipes the dusty paths clear again,
you might see the trails they've left –
one smooth line down the middle,
the mark of their sole achievement,
on either side, like stitches in the sand,
the tenuous wisps of two lumbering legs.

Robben Island

A tourist trap. The best part
is the boat ride over –
though the water is always rough
and by the time we got there
half of us were breathing deep,
sweat beading our foreheads.
From the boat, right onto a bus –
tour guide working from a script.
A drive around the island –
everything that would be interesting
too far to see clearly through
the smudged, plexiglass windows –
and we are not allowed to wander.
Finally off the bus, we enter
the prison. They assemble us
in a long concrete room. I stand next
to the one metal bunk they've left up
to illustrate the material hardships
conferred upon those held here.
An ex-inmate stands before us –
his remarks scripted as well.
He still cannot speak his mind.
He slept in this room for a decade
with barred windows open
to the elements, with no blankets.
He and fifty other men, who hacked
limestone in the quarry which reflected
the sun so brightly it blinded many,
would sing songs full of hope,
peace, and freedom … and now,
a cell phone rings – an awful pop song
echoes through the chamber.
A woman seems unembarrassed,
sifting through her shoulder bag,
in no apparent hurry to hit mute.

Continued

Speech over, a quick stroll through
a courtyard where the prisoners played
tennis and would slice balls open
with sharpened rocks, slip messages in
and lob them into other courtyards.
Finally, a walk past Mandela's cell –
mat on the floor, blankets folded,
three-legged stool, wooden bucket –
no time to loiter, back onto the boat.
And as we pull out and head to Capetown,
mulling over our disappointment, we tried
to find something worth taking away.
And as the island grew distant behind us,
I remember thinking, ever so briefly,
that when the bus stopped for refreshments
at the concession stand along the coast,
the whitewater foamed like rage
on the face of ten foot waves crashing
on the jagged rocks, wet and black.

Wine Tasting

The back of his neck folds like a cracked saddlebag,
a voice smooth as chipped granite, he regales us
with far-fetched stories of growing up in these hills.

It's only he and his wife at home – the children have left.
A soldier during apartheid, now retired, he shepherds
festive and well-paying tourists from vineyard to vineyard.

Sitting with us under a massive canopy of oak branches
nearly two centuries old, he mentions his son, the youngest –
"No work now for whites" he claims. His country has changed.

That voice catches. His red eyes darken, he excuses himself
to stroll along the waist-high stucco wall that separates us
from the vines. We sit and twirl our glasses in silence.

In a few years, when he finally clutches his chest,
collapses and exhales that last, extinguishing breath,
eight thousand miles from wherever I'll be –

will I notice something just slightly off, a fissure
in an otherwise normal day, as I sip a California red
and stroke my dog's snout until he closes his eyes?

Not knowing him well enough to argue or to comfort,
we regain our revelry over a crisp Chenin Blanc – I catch
the sun in the golden disc I tilt to the sharp lip of my glass.

The Long Flight Home

We take off in darkness, near midnight
and bank sharply over the lights of Johannesburg.
We're loaded down with whatever we need –
books, music, a bag of snacks and bottled water,
u-shaped pillows that wrap around our necks
and have just a little too much stuffing in them.
And because we are headed north and west,
back over the timelines we already crossed,
the hard oval frames that mark each aisle
will be black for the next sixteen hours.

The time inside us does not match the time
that ticks by on the face of my watch.
Three glasses of chardonnay and an Ambien –
that place between sleep and consciousness
I cannot name. We are traveling backwards –
Savannah, two nights before the wedding,
closing down that seafood place on River Street;
College, the Smokey Mountains at sun-up,
windows down, two joints and no deadlines.
Swimming pool, seventh grade, the flow
of water over sudden evolutionary curves.
Oversized yellow raincoat and rubber boots,
a steep hill in Sao Paulo, parents antiquing.

We take off in darkness, we land in darkness.
My wife shifts in her seat, the lights come on –
Atlanta burns in the distance outside our window.
The asphalt screeches the thick wheels into action.
We taxi; we file slowly; in a daze, we depart.
Outside of Customs, they give you a choice –
"Final Destination," or "Continuing Traveler."
Such decisions, and after so long a flight.
They have no idea what they do to us.

Where I Go When I Go for a Drive

Under the right circumstances –
which have nothing to do with planetary alignment,
but rather with soaring guitar solos, interwoven
by sunlight lances, the velvet flow of air
through rolled-down car windows
and the delicate arboreal slant
of a nameless road – you can eye-amble
down to a horse farm and a red barn house,
past a ceremonious, floral-lined walkway
to an old oak door with a pine wreath.
It's a sweater and jeans situation, and just before bed,
after the fire has again been expertly extinguished,
Mr. and Mrs. Red-Barn-Horse-Farm
hustle to get under the heavy covers,
shiver their way to sleep.

                        And if you follow
the familiar shape of that roof, 45 degrees
to skyward, off into the scattered cerulean,
you can look down at a different angle and wonder
who is riding on the freight trains in Montana,
creaking over passes in the Big Belts,
past five-story snow drifts – men in haggard leather
coats with fur liners are sharing a thermos
of strong coffee or hot chocolate, or better yet,
they're passing an engraved flask
of whiskey and remembering the "Frozen-Track
Winter of '71" and telling some young jackleg
how there were black nights when they thought
they wouldn't make it to breakfast.

Continued

                              Somehow, the far
side of that pass, just beyond the jagged horizon,
is an unknown street in downtown Tokyo
where a gaijin boy is entering a corner store –
a decrepit structure, ancient, surrounded
by modern behemoths with their neon scarves.
A goat's leg hangs from the ceiling, out in the open,
and other meats hurl a stench that burns
then fades like a rotten-egg sewer. The woman
behind the counter never smiles.

                              Several thousand miles
to the southwest, a thirty-something French couple
is scuba-ing and screwing their way through
a honeymoon, but she knows that in a week
she'll be back on her back for her coworker –
she doesn't hesitate to smile coy and sip her Pinot
and delicately finger the third button of her blouse.
In a non-descript suburb, a college sophomore
leans over a framed picture of his family,
exhales, then puts a straw into his nose.
And in Georgia, a car is hurtling down a country road,
windows down and the music playing far too loud,
in the driver's seat, a man grins, implodes.

The Snow-Bound House

I have only had one dream more than once,
and I remember, even at four, sweating
in my footed pajamas, that it felt
like something worth remembering.
And when I had the same dream again
on my 18th birthday, I obsessed over it –
rehashing, decoding, crafting alternate endings –
what could it mean that it came back?
Then again, tonight, I was there, standing
on the crest of a steep ridge, watching
the wind whip my breath away like gun smoke.
Below me, in a ragged shawl of pines –
a solitary house, snow bound, lit from within.
And every step like the clap of a distant rifle.

About the Author

Robert Pfeiffer attended Wake Forest University where he graduated with a Bachelor's Degree in English. After working on Capitol Hill for a year, he moved south, where he received his MFA and PhD in Creative Writing from Georgia State University. His poetry has appeared internationally in various journals and magazines as well as on WRAS Radio. He currently lives in Atlanta with his wife and their two dogs and teaches English at Clayton State University. This is his first collection of poems.

www.ingramcontent.com/pod-product-compliance
Lightning Source LLC
Chambersburg PA
CBHW052110070526
44584CB00017B/2420